MW00713434

For Lynn, who has been my very best friend since second grade. Love you lots. —Dena

♡

04 05 06 07 08 WKT 10 9 8 7 6 5 4 3 2 1

ISBN: 0-7407-4687-1

Book design by Julie Barnes

ATTENTION: SCHOOLS AND BUSINESSES

My Sweetest FRIEND

Recipes for the Perfect Friendship

By Dena™

Andrews McMeel Publishing

Kansas City

This little book is for everyone who is lucky
enough to have a special friend who makes life
a little easier... and a lot more fun.

A special friend is there
through the good and the bad.

Someone who listens and encourages...
who laughs with you and cries for you.

A friend who helps you pick up the pieces of your broken heart, holds your hand during the scary stuff, shares your best days—and helps you shop for that perfect outfit for a big date.

So pack your bags and let's get going! The cool convertible top is down and we're ready to roll, to head off on crazy adventures like only true friends can.

Thank you for being
that special friend.

♡

Everything
is more fun
when I share it
with you.

MOVIES

"A friend knows the song in
my *heart* and *sings* it
to me when my memory fails."

—Donna Roberts

Delish!

There's no better way to while a lazy day away than a long chat with you over a hot cup of java. Stolen moments perfect for getting down to the nitty-gritty about the important things... careers, boys, makeup, fashion, and anything sparkly, of course.

The Perfect Cup of Friendship Joe...

THE CAFÉ MOCHA

- Pour lots and lots of chocolate syrup at the bottom of a mug.

- Follow with a shot of espresso and steamed milk.

- Top off with whipped cream and a dusting of cocoa. *Delish!*

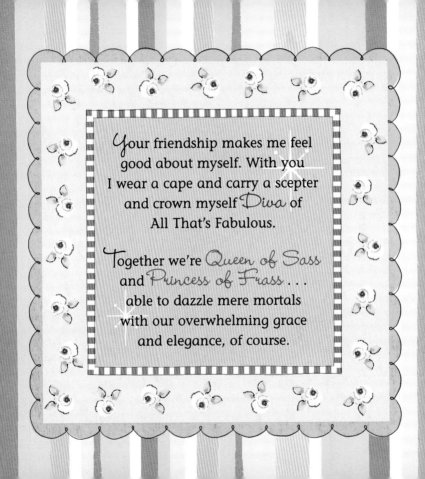

Your friendship makes me feel
good about myself. With you
I wear a cape and carry a scepter
and crown myself Diva of
All That's Fabulous.

Together we're Queen of Sass
and Princess of Frass . . .
able to dazzle mere mortals
with our overwhelming grace
and elegance, of course.

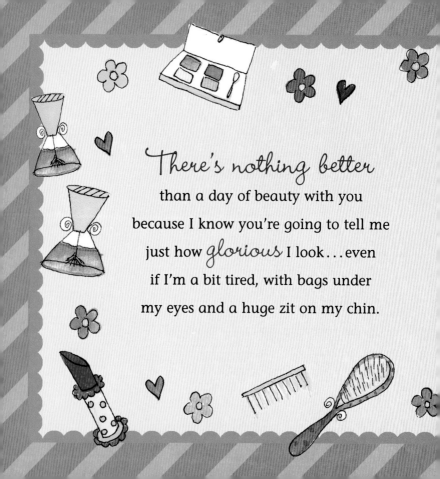

There's nothing better
than a day of beauty with you
because I know you're going to tell me
just how *glorious* I look...even
if I'm a bit tired, with bags under
my eyes and a huge zit on my chin.

Armed with the knowledge and
products of our inspirational sisters
(Trish McEvoy, Estée Lauder,
Bobbi Brown, and Coco Chanel,
of course!) we begin our quest to find the
poutiest lips, the sultriest eyes, and the
most chiseled cheekbones.

A rainy day
with you
brightens
my spirits.

It means I get to wear my high-fashion waterproof boots and gives me a great excuse to buy a new umbrella that perfectly matches my outfit.

In the rain we can tell each other our darkest secrets or greatest dreams.

Or we can just stomp through puddles and talk...without saying anything at all.

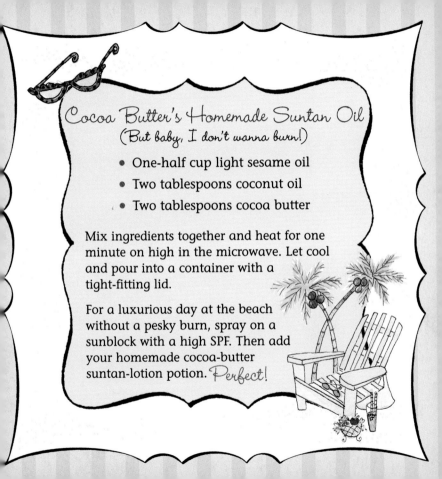

Cocoa Butter's Homemade Suntan Oil
(But baby, I don't wanna burn!)

- One-half cup light sesame oil
- Two tablespoons coconut oil
- Two tablespoons cocoa butter

Mix ingredients together and heat for one minute on high in the microwave. Let cool and pour into a container with a tight-fitting lid.

For a luxurious day at the beach without a pesky burn, spray on a sunblock with a high SPF. Then add your homemade cocoa-butter suntan-lotion potion. Perfect!

Remember our mother's mantra? "You can never be too rich or too thin." Well, Mom, you *can* be too thin. So how about this:

"You can never be too rich or have too many shoes and purses."

Fits us much better.

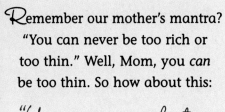

What every girl needs:

- That perfect little black dress . . .
- A string of pearls . . .
- Sexy jeans to wear to the movies . . .

- High heels that don't hurt your feet (at least not for a few hours)...

- And her own washer and dryer, of course.

I love tea for two with you! We wear our most fabulous hats and meet for high tea, with emphasis on presentation and conversation, of course!

Cucumber and Mint-Butter Tea Sandwiches

- Unsalted butter
- Fresh mint leaves, chopped
- Sliced wheat and white bread
- One cucumber, sliced thin
- Sugar

Soften butter and add fresh mint leaves. Spread butter mixture generously on bread. Top one slice of buttered bread with sliced cucumbers. Sprinkle a dash of sugar over cucumber. Top with another bread slice. Trim crusts and cut diagonally.

Sometimes being a good friend means admitting you've been a bad one.

I'm sorry

. . . for letting your life get away from me.

. . . for letting a boy come between us.

. . . for telling you all about me, and not asking all about you.

. . . for not being there when you needed me.

. . . for not being the friend to you that you are to me.

I'm sorry.

It's time we have a girls' night out...in!

THING TO DO:

- Take all the *Cosmo* quizzes only after you've read the results.

- Have a worthwhile makeover and wax the 'stache.

- Make real nachos (*without* the fat-free cheese) and eat the whole plate.

- Hope the boys *don't* come over for a panty raid so we can get to bed by ten!

There's nothing better than a nice long phone chat with a friend.

Think unloading the dishes while your favorite gal pal pours her heart out is appropriate? Think again.

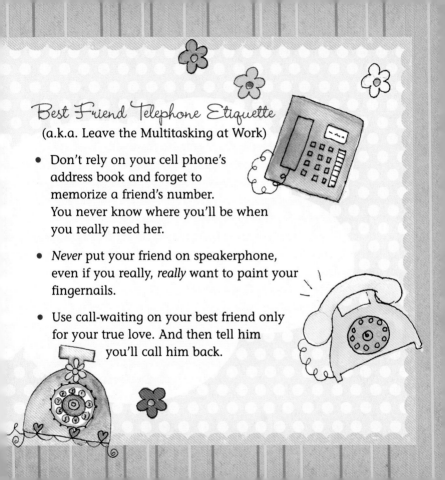

Best Friend Telephone Etiquette
(a.k.a. Leave the Multitasking at Work)

- Don't rely on your cell phone's address book and forget to memorize a friend's number. You never know where you'll be when you really need her.

- *Never* put your friend on speakerphone, even if you really, *really* want to paint your fingernails.

- Use call-waiting on your best friend only for your true love. And then tell him you'll call him back.

We are beautiful women.

"Plain women know more about
men than beautiful ones do.
But beautiful women don't need
to know about men. It's the men
who have to know about
beautiful women."

—Katharine Hepburn

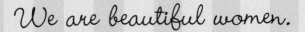

"The best mirror is an old friend."

—George Herbert

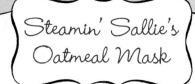

Steamin' Sallie's Oatmeal Mask

There's nothing better after a long day than a relaxing facial. So grab your friend and get glam, baby!

One-third cup oatmeal
One-half cup very warm water
Two tablespoons plain yogurt
Two tablespoons honey
One egg white

- Mix together oatmeal and water; set aside to thicken.
- Mix remaining ingredients together and add to oatmeal and water mixture.
- Spread over face, avoiding eyes.
- Spend the next fifteen minutes relaxing—listening to music, talking about shoes, or eating chocolates.
- Rinse with warm water and admire. *Luscious!*

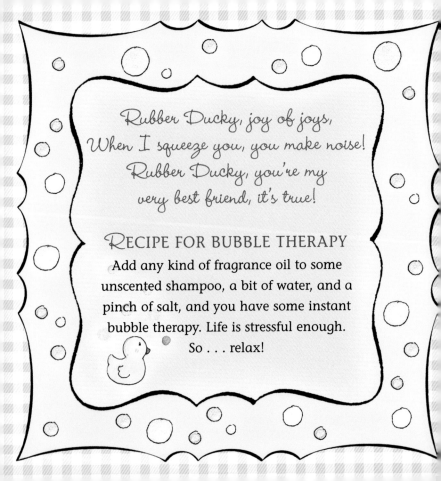

Rubber Ducky, joy of joys,
When I squeeze you, you make noise!
Rubber Ducky, you're my
very best friend, it's true!

RECIPE FOR BUBBLE THERAPY

Add any kind of fragrance oil to some
unscented shampoo, a bit of water, and a
pinch of salt, and you have some instant
bubble therapy. Life is stressful enough.
So . . . relax!

SHOP!

I've found out it's
fun to go shopping.
It's such a feminine
thing to do.

—Marilyn Monroe

A friend is the
only person you
can dump your
purse in front of!

In her purse, every successful woman should have:

- that perfect tube of lipstick
- a fully charged cell phone (natch!)
- a little bit of cash for a sandwich on the go
- a credit card for that perfect pair of shoes
- a discreet tin of after-coffee mints
- . . . and some Kleenex for when you laugh so hard you cry!

Mimi's Sticky Fudge

IN A PAN, MELT:

1 c. sugar • Two squares
unsweetened baker's chocolate
• 1 $\frac{1}{2}$ T. Karo syrup • $\frac{1}{4}$ c. milk
• 1 T. butter • Splash of vanilla

Boil for about a minute
for sticky fudge...boil
for two minutes for
supersticky fudge!

Pour over ice cream
and share with a friend!

And as this little book comes to a close,
you are indeed my sweetest friend.

As Emily Dickinson put it,

"My friends
are my estate."

But I prefer Pooh's outlook:

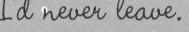

"Promise you won't forget me, because if I thought you would, I'd never leave."